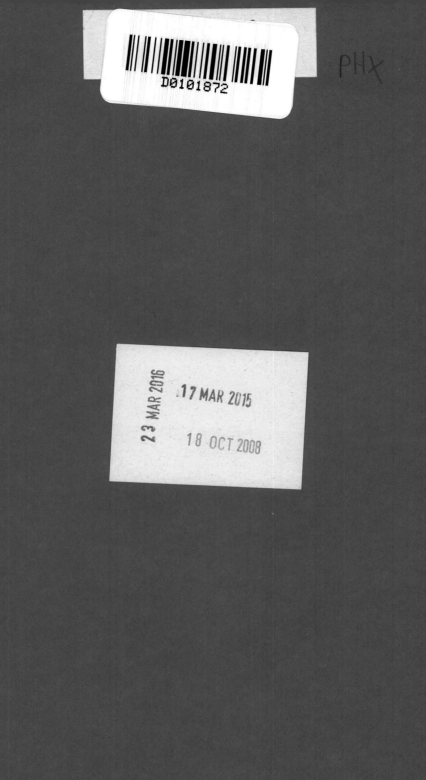

EGYPT

LETTERS FROM AROUND THE WORLD

David Cumming

Photographs by Howard Davies

CHERRYTREE BOOKS

LETTERS FROM AROUND THE WORLD

Titles in this series

AUSTRALIA • BANGLADESH • BRAZIL • CANADA • CHINA • COSTA RICA
EGYPT • FRANCE • GERMANY • GREECE • INDIA • INDONESIA • ITALY
JAMAICA • JAPAN • KENYA • MEXICO • PAKISTAN • SOUTH AFRICA • SPAIN

A Cherrytree Book

Conceived and produced by

Nutshell MEDIA

Intergen House
65-67 Western Road
Hove BN3 2JQ, UK
www.nutshellmedialtd.co.uk

First published in 2005 by
Evans Brothers Ltd
2A Portman Mansions
Chiltern Street
London W1U 6NR

VISIT OUR WEBSITE
www.evansbooks.co.uk

Editor: Polly Goodman
Design: Mayer Media Ltd
Map artwork: Encompass Graphics Ltd
All other artwork: Mayer Media Ltd

All photographs are by Howard Davies.

Acknowledgements
The photographer would like to thank Esraa Masry and
her family, the staff and pupils of Rahebat Primary
School, Luxor, Tarek Sidky and the Touring Club of
Egypt, Nashwa Hamid at the Egypt Embassy, and Ahmed
Mostafa and the Cairo Press Centre for all their help.

British Library Cataloguing in Publication Data
Cumming, David, 1953–
   Egypt. – (Letters from around the world)
   1. Egypt – Social conditions – 1981 – Juvenile
   literature
   2. Egypt – Social life and customs – 21st century –
   Juvenile literature
   I. Title
962'.055

ISBN 1 84234 276 2

Cover: Esraa (back left) with her younger brother
Karim (front right) and two friends beside the River
Nile, in Luxor.
Title page: Esraa (centre) playing with her classmates
during the mid-morning break at school.
This page: Luxor temple with the city behind.
Contents page: Esraa looks down on the street below
from the balcony of her flat.
Glossary page: Esraa doing her English homework.
Further Information page: In Ancient Egypt, when
important people died their bodies were mummified and
put into cases, like this one in a Luxor museum.
Index: One of the famous pyramids at Giza, near Cairo.

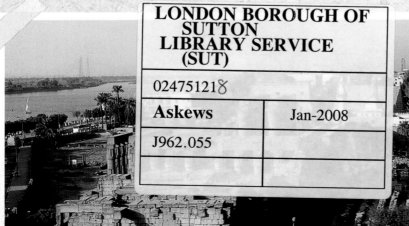

Contents

My Country

Tuesday, 9 September

Flat 3
91 Nile River Road
Luxor
Egypt

Dear Jackie,

Salaam Aleikum! (You say 'Sa-lam Alay-kum'. This means 'hello' in Arabic, my language.)

My name is Esraa Masry. I'm 9 years old and I live in Luxor, in Egypt. I've got two brothers, Mohamed, who's 14 and Karim, who is 6. Do you have any brothers and sisters?

If you want any information on Egypt, write back and ask me.

From
Esraa

Here I am with my parents and brothers, on the balcony of our flat. →

People have lived in Egypt for thousands of years. The Ancient Egyptians built huge towns and temples. The remains can still be seen today, 4,000 years later.

Egypt's place in the world.

Egypt is in the Middle East, in the north-east corner of Africa. The River Nile flows northwards into the Mediterranean Sea.

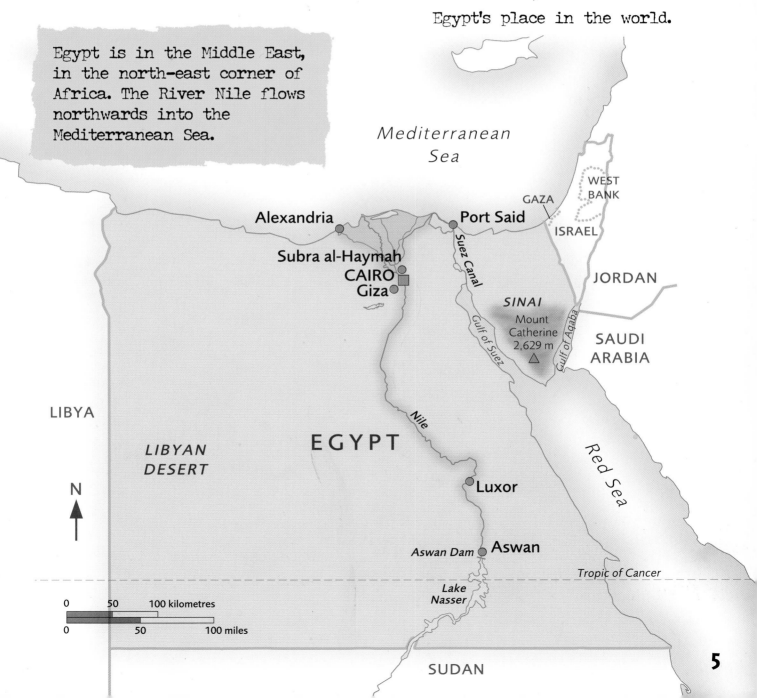

Mediterranean Sea

WEST BANK

GAZA

Alexandria

Port Said

ISRAEL

Subra al-Haymah

CAIRO

Giza

JORDAN

Suez Canal

SINAI

Mount Catherine 2,629 m

Gulf of Suez

Gulf of Aqaba

SAUDI ARABIA

LIBYA

LIBYAN DESERT

EGYPT

Nile

Red Sea

N

Luxor

Aswan Dam

Aswan

Tropic of Cancer

Lake Nasser

0   50   100 kilometres

0   50   100 miles

SUDAN

Luxor is beside the River Nile. About 150,000 people live there today. Luxor grew up among the ruins of Thebes, an important city in Ancient Egypt. Tourists come from all over the world to look at the remains of Thebes.

These are the remains of the ancient temple in the centre of Luxor. Work began on it in about 1400 BC. You can see the River Nile on the left.

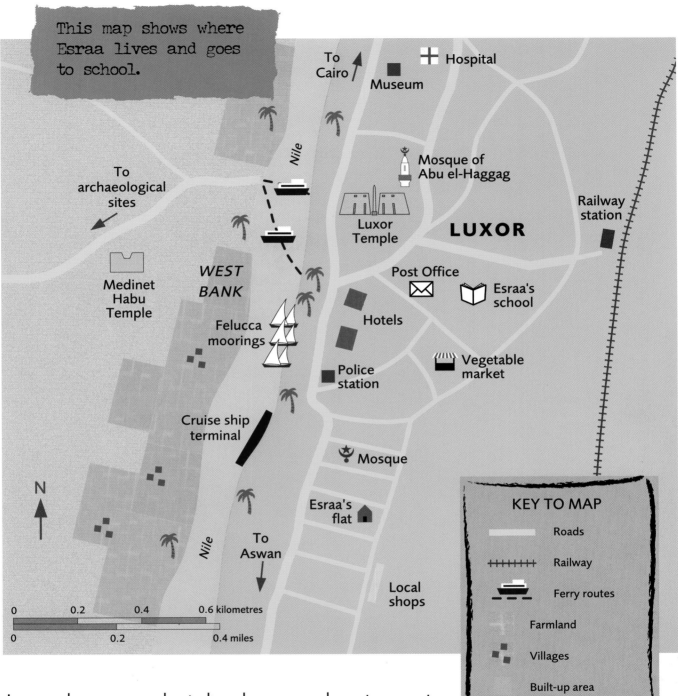

This map shows where Esraa lives and goes to school.

To Cairo

Hospital

Museum

Mosque of Abu el-Haggag

To archaeological sites

Nile

Railway station

Luxor Temple

LUXOR

Medinet Habu Temple

WEST BANK

Post Office

Esraa's school

Hotels

Felucca moorings

Vegetable market

Police station

Cruise ship terminal

Mosque

N

Nile

To Aswan

Esraa's flat

Local shops

KEY TO MAP

	Roads
+++++++	Railway
	Ferry routes
	Farmland
	Villages
	Built-up area

0   0.2   0.4   0.6 kilometres

0   0.2   0.4 miles

Luxor has many hotels, shops and restaurants
that are used by the tourists. Most of these
are along the Nile, near the dock of the cruise ships.
These ships take visitors to Aswan, stopping at ruins
on the way.

Landscape and Weather

Much of Egypt is a sandy desert, where no one lives and little grows. Nearly 99 per cent of the people live beside the River Nile. Here, crops can be grown using water from the river. The Nile also provides people with water for drinking and for washing.

The Nile is an important transport route. Modern cruise ships and traditional feluccas travel up and down the river.

Egypt has a desert climate. The summers are hot and the winters are warm. Hardly any rain falls throughout the year.

Egypt is 96 per cent desert. This pyramid is on the edge of the Libyan Desert at Giza, near Cairo.

Luxor's Climate

January

Temperature

14°C

6mm

Rainfall

July

Temperature

35°C

1mm

Rainfall

At Home

Like most people in Luxor, Esraa lives in a flat. It is about 1 kilometre from the city centre (see map on page 7). The flat is on the third floor. It has a balcony overlooking the street. The balcony is useful for drying washing. Clothes dry quickly, especially during the hot summer.

Esraa likes to watch the street below from the balcony of her flat.

The fan is used in the hot summer months to keep the living-room cool.

The flat has a large, airy living-room where there is a TV, a video recorder and an electric keyboard. Esraa's dad is teaching the children how to play it. There is also a small kitchen with a cooker and fridge, a bathroom and three bedrooms.

Foreign TV programmes have Arabic subtitles, which Esraa can follow.

Esraa likes helping her mum with the cooking and learning how to make meals.

Esraa has her own bedroom, while Karim and Mohamed share one. Esraa has a computer in her bedroom, but all the family use it.

Esraa and Karim play a game on the computer in Esraa's bedroom.

Wednesday, 24 September

Flat 3
91 Nile River Road
Luxor
Egypt

Dear Jackie,

Thanks for your letter. You asked about Arabic writing. Well, it may look like lots of funny squiggles to you, but it's actually different letters joined together. There are 18 letters in Arabic writing. We can add dots above or below some of them to give us another 10 letters, so altogether there are 28 letters in our alphabet. It was strange reading your letter from left to right because we read and write Arabic from right to left. So when we open a book, we start at what you would call the last page!

Write back soon.

From

Esraa

Here I am writing Arabic for my homework.

Food and Mealtimes

For breakfast, Esraa has sweet tea with bread, butter and jam. For lunch, she usually has *kushari*. This is a tasty mixture of noodles, rice, macaroni, lentils and onions in a spicy tomato sauce.

Esraa's family eat mainly vegetables, and pulses such as beans and lentils. They also eat a little meat, but being Muslims, they are not allowed to eat pork. Sometimes they have fresh fish from the River Nile.

Esraa and her family always have dinner together, usually at about 8 p.m. Here they are eating felafels and salads with some bread.

Esraa and Karim
help their father
to buy vegetables
for dinner.

The family buy their food fresh every day from local
shops and street sellers. Once a week, Esraa's father
goes to a supermarket or Luxor's main vegetable market
to buy things he can't get locally.

The local baker has
a wide selection of
fresh bread cooked
that morning.

All sorts of fruit and vegetables are grown in the fields on the west bank of the Nile. Sugar cane, tomatoes, onions, oranges and dates are some of the many crops farmed there.

Esraa prepares a salad with fresh vegetables bought from the market.

Thursday, 9 October

Flat 3
91 Nile River Road
Luxor
Egypt

Hi Jackie,

Here's a recipe for my favourite snack – felafel:

You will need: 1 tin of chickpeas, 1 onion, 1 garlic clove, 1 teaspoon of cumin powder, 4 tablespoons of vegetable oil, some flour, pinch of pepper and salt.

1. Chop up the onion, garlic and chickpeas in a food processor.
2. Empty them into a bowl and mix in the cumin, salt and pepper.
3. Make small balls out of the mixture and roll them in the flour.
4. Heat the oil in a frying pan and fry the felafels, turning when golden brown.

Write and tell me what you think.

Esraa

Here are some felafels I made, with salad and pitta bread.

School Day

Esraa waits for a service taxi to take her to school.

Esraa goes to school in the centre of Luxor (see map on page 7). She leaves for school at 7 a.m. It takes her about 10 minutes to get there by a 'service taxi'. This is a car or minibus that picks up and drops passengers along its route.

Every morning at assembly, the pupils sing the national anthem and salute the Egyptian flag.

School starts at 8 a.m. with assembly and finishes at 1.30 p.m. Esraa usually has seven classes a day. She studies Arabic, English, geography, maths, science, art and social studies. There are no classes on Fridays, the Muslim holy day, or Sundays.

Esraa reads out loud to the class in an Arabic reading lesson.

At the mid-morning break, the children eat snacks in the courtyard outside.

Esraa started school when she was 6 years old. When she is 12, she will go to middle school until she is 14. Then she will start at Luxor Secondary School for Girls. Afterwards she wants to go to medical school in Cairo to become a doctor.

Esraa goes to an all-girls school. Girls and boys are taught separately in Muslim countries like Egypt.

Friday, 24 October

Flat 3
91 Nile River Road
Luxor
Egypt

Hi Jackie,

I'm glad you liked the felafels.

So you play in the school band too! I love playing in ours.
We've got an electronic keyboard, which two people play.
The rest of us play triangles, maraccas and a drum.
Sometimes we play at assembly. We have to concentrate
really hard to stay in time, otherwise my friends giggle!

Write back soon.

From

Esraa

Here's my school band,
playing at assembly.

Off to Work

Tourism is the most important industry in Egypt. Esraa's father works for a travel agency in Luxor, looking after visitors.

This man earns money from letting tourists ride his camel in the desert near Aswan.

City people like this street seller often have several part-time jobs because work is difficult to find.

Many Egyptians earn a living from agriculture. Cotton is one of the main crops grown. Egyptian cotton is said to be the best in the world.

In Cairo, there are factories making cotton into clothes and towels. Cars are also made in Cairo. On the Red Sea, a new industry is starting up – drilling for natural gas.

About a third of Egyptians are farmers. Most of them only have a little land and a few animals.

Free Time

Esraa likes to watch TV, read, and play computer games. She and her brothers meet their friends to kick a ball about in the streets or ride their bikes.

For their holidays, Esraa and her family go to Cairo or Aswan to visit their grandparents.

Feluccas have been used for fishing and transport on the Nile for thousands of years. Today they are mainly used to take people on river trips.

These children are playing on the River Nile near Luxor, in boats they have made from old canoes.

Saturday, 8 November

Flat 3
91 Nile River Road
Luxor
Egypt

Hi Jackie,

My dad was born on an island in the River Nile, at Aswan. His relatives still live there, so we go down there on our holidays to see my grandparents, uncles and aunts. It takes about 4 hours to get there by train. My dad's friend Mostafa usually takes us out on his felucca. It's got a huge triangular sail and a flat bottom. It's wide too, and can carry up to 20 people. It's lovely going for a sail at sunset.

From

Esraa

Here's Mostafa, taking us out for a sail on his felucca.

Religion

Most people in Egypt are Muslim. Every Friday, the Muslim holy day, Esraa's father goes to the local mosque for midday prayers. When they were younger, Esraa and her brothers used to go to a *madrassa* (mosque school), where they learned about the Qur'an, the Muslim holy book.

These boys are learning the Qur'an at a *madrassa* in Luxor.

This man is selling children's musical instruments for the festival of Abu el-Haggag.

Every year Esraa looks forward to the Muslim festivals, especially the festival of Abu el-Haggag. This is held in honour of a Muslim holy man who lived in Luxor 800 years ago. There are noisy parades, stick fights and horse races, as well as singing and dancing.

At the festival of Abu el-Haggag, there are displays of stick fighting. It's only pretend fighting and no one gets hurt.

27

Fact File

Flag: The Egyptian flag is split into three equal strips of red (top), white and black. In the middle of the white strip there is a gold eagle.

Capital city: Cairo. With a population of about 15 million people, Cairo is by far the biggest city in Africa. The city is very overcrowded, with many people living in crowded slums.

Other major cities: Alexandria, Aswan, Giza, Luxor, Port Said and Subra al-Haymah.

Population: 76.1 million.

Size: 1,001,450 km².

Languages: Arabic, English, French.

Main industries: Tourism, textiles, food processing, chemicals.

Currency: Egyptian pound (divided into piastres). 1 Egyptian pound = 100 piastres. Egyptian pound notes have Arabic and English writing on them.

History: One of the world's greatest civilizations developed in Egypt between 3100 and 1085 BC. Its people, the Ancient Egyptians, built enormous temples, tombs and towns. They developed a system of writing using signs and symbols, called hieroglyphics (below).

Famous monuments: The Pyramids of Giza are one of the Seven Wonders of the World – famous buildings and sculpture from ancient times. The pyramids were tombs for the pharaohs (kings).

Highest point: Mount Catherine (2,629m).

Longest river: Nile (6,738km), which is also the longest river in the world.

Main religions: About 94 per cent of Egyptians are Muslims. Most other people are Christians.

Main festivals: Ramadan, Eid el-Fitr, Eid el-Adha and Moulid el-Nabi are the main Islamic festivals. Sham el-Nessim (Easter Monday) is the main Christian festival.

Famous people: Boutros Boutros-Ghali (born 1922) was head of the United Nations between 1992 and 1996; Naguib Mahfouz (born 1911) is a Nobel Prize-winning novelist and screenplay writer.

Stamps: Some of the best stamps show people and monuments from Ancient Egypt.

Glossary

Ancient Egypt One of the world's first civilizations, which developed in Egypt between 3100–1085 BC.

Arabic One of several similar languages spoken in Egypt, Iraq, Saudi Arabia, Syria, Lebanon, Jordan and North Africa.

BC Short for 'Before Christ'. This means the number of years before the birth of Jesus Christ.

civilizations Peoples who have organized their countries well.

climate The normal weather in a place.

crop Food grown by farmers.

desert A large area of very dry, dusty land.

feluccas Flat-bottomed sailing boats with a triangular sail.

irrigate To supply land with water so that crops can grow.

madrassa A school attached to a mosque, where the pupils learn about Islam.

mosque A building in which Muslims pray.

mummified Treated with preservatives before burial.

Muslims Followers of Islam.

pulses The edible seeds (like peas, beans and lentils) of some plants.

pyramid A huge, four-sided pointed tomb in which the Ancient Egyptians buried important people.

Qur'an The holy book of Islam.

remains Ruins left over from times long ago.

slums Overcrowded parts of cities, often with unhealthy conditions.

subtitles Writing on a film or TV screen so that viewers can understand foreign films or programmes.

temple A place for worship.

Further Information

Information books:

Changing Face of Egypt by Ron Ragsdale (Hodder Wayland, 2002)

Encyclopedia of Ancient Egypt (Usborne, 2004)

Gods and Goddesses of Ancient Egypt by Leon Ashworth (Cherrytree Books, 2001)

River Journey: Nile by Rob Bowden (Hodder Wayland, 2003)

World of Recipes: Egypt by Sue Townsend & Caroline Young (Heinemann, 2004)

Fiction:

The Orchard Book of Stories from Ancient Egypt by Robert Swindells (Orchard Books, 2003)

Stories from Ancient Civilisations: Egypt by Shahrukh Husain (Evans, 2003)

Resource packs:

Action Pack: Pyramid (Dorling Kindersley, 2003)

Websites:

Guardian's Egypt
www.guardians.net/egypt/
Includes a virtual tour of the pyramids, with many links.

Egyptology On Line
www.egyptologyonline.com/
Information on Ancient Egypt, including the pyramids, religion and famous pharaohs.

Egypt Links
ce.eng.usf.edu/pharos/
Links to websites about Egypt, both past and present.

Index